An Apple a Day

Treasured Selections from *Apples of Gold*

by Jo Petty

The C.R.Gibson Company
Norwalk, Connecticut

A word fitly spoken
is like apples of gold
in pictures of silver.

Proverbs 25:11

January 1
Each new day is an opportunity to start all over again
. . . to cleanse our minds and hearts anew and to clarify
our vision. And let us not clutter up today with the
leavings of other days.

January 2
It is when the holiday is over that we begin to enjoy it.

January 3
Dare to be wise; begin! He who postpones the hour of
living rightly is like the rustic who waits for the river to
run out before he crosses.

January 4
If you never stick your neck out, you'll never get your
head above the crowd.

January 5
Resolve to be better for the echo of it.

January 6
Plan your work—work your plan.

January 7
The past cannot be changed; the future is still in your
power.

January 8
To do the right thing for the wrong reason is the greatest
treason.

January 9
The worst bankrupt in the world is the man who has lost
his enthusiasm. Let him lose everything but enthusiasm
and he will come through again to success.

January 10
Life is a voyage in which we choose neither vessel nor weather, but much can be done in the management of the sails and the guidance of the helm.

January 11
The more difficult the obstacle, the stronger one becomes after hurdling it.

January 12
The real purpose of our existence is not to make a living, but to make a life—a worthy, well-rounded, useful life.

January 13
Life is 10% what you make it and 90% how you take it.

January 14
Some men have their first dollar. The man who is really rich is one who still has his first friend.

January 15
That man is the richest whose pleasures are the cheapest.

January 16
An admission of error is a sign of strength rather than a confession of weakness.

January 17
A good man does not hesitate to own he has been in the wrong. He takes comfort in knowing he is wiser today than he was yesterday.

January 18
No life ever grows great until it is focused, dedicated, disciplined.

January 19
Goodness is the only investment that never fails.

January 20
The greatest distance we have yet to cover still lies within us.

January 21
Habit is a cable; we weave a thread of it every day, and at last we cannot break it.

January 22
As easy as falling off a diet.

January 23
Overweight is often just desserts.

January 24
A friend is one who knows all about you and still likes you.

January 25
Seconds count, especially when dieting.

January 26
Will Power—Won't Power—Supreme Power!

January 27
To cease smoking is the easiest thing I ever did. I ought to know for I've done it a thousand times.

January 28
Will power is the ability to eat one salted peanut.

January 29
The best victory is to conquer self.

January 30
He who influences the thought of his time influences the thought of all the times that follow.

January 31
The rest of our days depends upon the rest of our nights.

February 1
Happiness consists in activity—it is a running stream, not a stagnant pool.

February 2
The only way on earth to multiply happiness is to divide it.

February 3
Friendship is to be purchased only by friendship.

February 4
Real friends are those who, when you've made a fool of yourself, don't feel that you've done a permanent job.

February 5
An open mind leaves a chance for someone to drop a worthwhile thought in it.

February 6
Every man's work is a portrait of himself.

February 7
A friend is a person with whom you dare to be yourself.

February 8
Anyone can carry his burden, however heavy, until nightfall; anyone can do his work, however hard, for one day.

February 9
Friendship is the only cement that will ever hold the world together.

February 10
Character is property—it is the noblest of possessions.

February 11
The best gifts are tied with heartstrings.

February 12
Love sees through a telescope—not a microscope.

February 13
The door to the human heart can be opened only from the inside.

February 14
The best and most beautiful things in the world cannot be seen nor touched but are felt in the heart.

February 15
We like someone because. We love someone although.

February 16
Love cannot be wasted. It makes no difference where it is bestowed, it always brings in big returns.

February 17
It also takes two to make up after a quarrel.

February 18
Faults are thick when love is thin.

February 19
Try to fix the mistake—never the blame.

February 20
Today is the tomorrow you worried about yesterday.

February 21
To be without some of the things you want is an indispensable part of happiness.

February 22
I had no shoes and complained until I met a man who had no feet.

February 23
Don't tell me that worry doesn't do any good. I know better. The things I worry about don't happen.

February 24
To see God in everything makes life the greatest adventure there is.

February 25
Things are pretty well evened up in this world. Other people's troubles are not so bad as yours, but their children are a lot worse.

February 26
Before you flare up at anyone's faults, take time to count ten—ten of your own.

February 27
The difference between a prejudice and a conviction is that you can explain a conviction without getting mad.

February 28
Dignity is the capacity to hold back on the tongue what never should have been in the mind in the first place.

March 1
Better to let 'em wonder why you didn't talk than why you did.

March 2
The secret of patience is doing something else in the meanwhile.

March 3
Do you see *difficulties* in every *opportunity* or *opportunities* in every *difficulty?*

March 4
Conscience is the still small voice that makes you feel still smaller.

March 5
First do more than you are paid for before expecting to be paid for more than you do.

March 6
He who loses money loses much; he who loses a friend loses more, but he who loses *faith* loses all.

March 7
Many of us spend half our time wishing for things we could have if we didn't spend half our time wishing.

March 8
When you get to the end of your rope, tie a knot in it and hang on.

March 9
The only conquests which are permanent, and leave no regrets, are conquests over ourselves.

March 10
Every time you give another a 'piece of your mind' you add to your own vacuum.

March 11
Anger is a wind which blows out the lamp of the mind.

March 12
When the archer misses the center of the target he seeks for the cause within himself.

March 13
Help me never to judge another until I have walked two weeks in his shoes.

March 14
So many Gods, so many creeds,
So many paths that wind and wind;
When just the art of being kind
Is all the sad world needs.

March 15
Do the very best you can . . . and leave the outcome to God.

March 16
With God, nothing shall be impossible.

March 17
The kindly word that falls today may bear its fruit tomorrow.

March 18
Cold and reserved natures should remember that, though not infrequently flowers may be found beneath the snow, it is chilly work to dig for them and few care to take the trouble.

March 19
If I keep a green bough in my heart, the singing bird will come.

March 20
Winter on her head—eternal spring in her heart.

March 21
Better to light one candle than to curse the darkness.

March 22
A candle-glow can pierce the darkest night.

March 23
No man ever injured his eyesight by looking on the bright side of things.

March 24
Sympathy is never wasted except when you give it to yourself.

March 25
We cannot do everything at once; but we can do something at once.

March 26
The only wise speed at which to live is . . . Godspeed.

March 27
See each person you meet as one who knows your Lord or is seeking your Lord.

March 28
We can easily forgive a child who is afraid of the dark. The real tragedy of life is when men are afraid of the Light.

March 29
The highest reward that God gives us for good work is
the ability to do better.

March 30
Who worships Christ in bread and wine,
And kneels before the High and Pure,
Meets Him again in street and mine
And in the faces of the poor.

March 31
Fear God and all other fears will disappear.

April 1
We can do anything we want if we stick to it long enough.

April 2
What counts is not the number of hours you put in, but
how much you put in the hours.

April 3
We always have time enough if we but use it aright.

April 4
Adolescence is the age at which children stop asking
questions because they know all the answers.

April 5
He didn't know it couldn't be done but went ahead and
did it.

April 6
There is no cosmetic for beauty like *happiness*.

April 7
Where love is, there God is.

April 8
The bird with a broken pinion never soared so high
again, but its song is sweeter!

April 9
It takes both rain and sunshine to make a rainbow.

April 10
You can't get anywhere today if you are still mired down
in yesterday.

April 11
Just think how happy you'd be if you lost everything you
have right now—and then got it back again.

April 12
So long as enthusiasm lasts, so long is youth still with us.

April 13
Not even the perpetually hungry live by bread alone.

April 14
Life is hard, by the yard;
But by the inch, *life's* a cinch!

April 15
Taxes could be much worse—suppose we had to pay on
what we *think* we're worth.

April 16
If your outgo exceeds your income, then your upkeep will
be your downfall.

April 17
Money may not go as far as it used to, but we have
just as much trouble getting it back.

April 18
Do you spend more than you make on things you don't need to impress people you don't like?

April 19
One of the hardest things to teach our children about money matters is that it does.

April 20
Little and often fills the purse.

April 21
Happiness is not a station you arrive at, but a manner of traveling.

April 22
Success is getting what you want;
Happiness is wanting what you get.

April 23
The secret of prayer is secret prayer.

April 24
Prayer is not a substitute for work. It is a desperate effort to work further and to be effective beyond the range of one's power.

April 25
To handle yourself, use your head;
To handle others, use your heart.

April 26
The only way to have a friend is to be one.

April 27
Do you have invisible means of support?

April 28
Tolerance comes with age. I see no fault committed that I myself could not have committed at some time or other.

April 29
Christian character is not an inheritance; each individual must build it for himself.

April 30
The smallest good deed is better than the grandest intention.

May 1
All the flowers of all the tomorrows are in the seeds of today.

May 2
My part is to improve the present moment.

May 3
What sunshine is to flowers, smiles are to humanity.

May 4
Life lived just to satisfy yourself never satisfies anybody.

May 5
He who would have nothing to do with thorns must never attempt to gather flowers.

May 6
Some cause happiness wherever they go; others whenever they go.

May 7
A good memory is fine—but the ability to forget is the true test of greatness.

May 8
Your body is for use—not abuse.

May 9
Meditation or Medication?

May 10
Do right and leave the results with God.

May 11
You can never tell about a woman, and if you can, you shouldn't.

May 12
God pardons like a mother, who kisses the offense into everlasting forgetfulness.

May 13
Mothers, as well as fools, sometimes walk where angels fear to tread.

May 14
A partnership with God is motherhood.

May 15
The father is the head of the house—
The mother is the heart of the house.

May 16
He drew a circle that shut me out,
But love and I had the wit to win;
We drew a larger circle that took him in.

May 17
Any housewife, no matter how large her family, can always get some time to be alone by doing the dishes.

May 18
Housework is something you do that nobody notices unless you don't do it.

May 19
Children need models more than they need critics.

May 20
Women will remain the weaker sex just as long as they're smarter.

May 21
It isn't the mountain ahead that wears you out—it's the grain of sand in your shoe.

May 22
Life is not the wick or the candle—it is the burning.

May 23
Inexperience is what makes a young man do what an older man says is impossible.

May 24
When you're through changing, you're through.

May 25
Never miss an opportunity to make others happy, even if you have to let them alone to do it.

May 26
To every man there opens a high way and a low and every man decides the way that he shall go.

May 27
There is no sense in advertising your troubles. There's no market for them.

May 28
The greatest of faults is to be conscious of none.

May 29
Some people can see at a glance what others cannot see with searchlights and telescopes.

May 30
God's requirements are met by God's enablings.

May 31
Life is too short to be little.

June 1
Success in marriage is much more than finding the right person; it is a matter of being the right person.

June 2
The bonds of matrimony aren't worth much unless the interest is kept up.

June 3
One of the mysteries of life is how the boy who wasn't good enough to marry the daughter can be the father of the smartest grandchild in the world.

June 4
I married her because we have so many faults in common.

June 5
The way to be happy is to make others happy.

June 6
A mistake at least proves somebody stopped talking long enough to do something.

June 7
The only greatness is unselfish love.

June 8
'Twas her thinking of others made you think of her.

June 9
A man's best fortune or his worst is his wife.

June 10
A woman worries about the future until she gets a husband, while a man never worries about the future until he gets a wife.

June 11
Why must we have memory enough to recall to the tiniest detail what has happened to us, and not enough to remember how many times we have told it to the same person?

June 12
Put yourself in his place.

June 13
Marrying is not Marriage.

June 14
The most difficult year of marriage is the one you're in.

June 15
The only way to settle a disagreement is on the basis of what's right—not who's right.

June 16
Flattery is something nice someone tells you about yourself that you wish were true.

June 17
We would rather be ruined by praise than saved by criticism.

June 18
Discussion is an exchange of knowledge: argument is an exchange of ignorance.

June 19
If you had to do it over, would you fall in love with yourself again?

June 20
It is only the forgiving who are qualified to receive forgiveness.

June 21
You shall judge a man by his foes as well as by his friends.

June 22
Truth is the foundation of all knowledge and the cement of all societies.

June 23
A little thing is a little thing, but faithfulness in little things is a great thing.

June 24
Kindness is a language the dumb can speak and the deaf understand.

June 25
You have no more right to consume happiness without producing it than to consume wealth without producing it.

June 26
Every calling is great when greatly pursued.

June 27
Restraint without love is barbarity. Love without restraint commits suicide.

June 28
Your friend has a friend, and your friend's friend has a friend; be discreet.

June 29
He who has learned to disagree without being disagreeable has discovered the most valuable secret of a diplomat.

June 30
The driver is safer when the roads are dry; the roads are safer when the driver is dry.

July 1
Liberty is always dangerous, but it is the safest thing we have.

July 2
To what avail the plow or sail, or land, or life, if freedom fail?

July 3
If there is no way out, there is a way up.

July 4
American Creed: Patriotism which leaps over the fence of party prejudice. Religion which jumps over the wall of intolerance. Brotherhood which climbs over the mountain of national separations.

July 5
Success is a bright sun that obscures and makes ridiculously unimportant all the little shadowy flecks of failure.

July 6
Man's capacity for justice makes democracy possible; but man's inclination to injustice makes democracy necessary.

July 7
Fine eloquence consists in saying all that should be, not all that could be said.

July 8
The office of government is not to confer happiness, but to give men opportunity to work out happiness for themselves.

July 9
If you must doubt, doubt your doubts—never your beliefs.

July 10
If you clutter up your mind with little things, will there be any room left for the big things?

July 11
Everyone is ignorant—only on different subjects.

July 12
Don't let the seeds spoil your enjoyment of a watermelon. Just spit out the seeds.

July 13
It's smart to pick your friends—but not to pieces.

July 14
Our country, right or wrong! When right, to be kept
right; when wrong, to be put right.

July 15
Democracy means not 'I am equal to you' but 'you are
equal to me.'

July 16
Nothing which is morally wrong can ever be politically
right.

July 17
We must be willing to pay a price for freedom, for no
price that is ever asked for it is half the cost of doing
without it.

July 18
The world belongs to the enthusiast who keeps cool.

July 19
The longer you keep your temper the more it will
improve.

July 20
Why is it opportunities always look bigger going than
coming?

July 21
Nothing is all wrong. Even a clock that has stopped
running is right twice a day.

July 22
Except in occasional emergencies there is not much that
one man can do for another, other than to help him to
help himself.

July 23
It is indeed a desirable thing to be well descended, but the glory belongs to our ancestors.

July 24
A clean conscience is a soft pillow.

July 25
Morale is when your hands and feet keep on working when your head says it can't be done.

July 26
You can't keep trouble from coming, but you needn't give it a chair to sit on.

July 27
Choose the best life, for habit will make it pleasant.

July 28
Be a lamp in the chamber if you cannot be a star in the sky.

July 29
It is easy to be pleasant
When life flows by like a song,
But the man worth while is one who will smile,
When everything goes dead wrong.

July 30
One of the great arts of living is the art of forgetting.

July 31
Be what you wish others to become.

August 1
What I am to be I am now becoming.

August 2
Keep your enthusiasms, and forget your birthdays—
formula for youth!

August 3
Swallowing your pride occasionally will never give you
indigestion.

August 4
Optimist or pessimist? Do you call traffic signals
go-lights?

August 5
It is with narrow-souled people as with narrow-necked
bottles—the less they have in them the more noise they
make in pouring it out.

August 6
Don't drive as if you own the road; drive as if you own
the car.

August 7
Though we travel the world over to find the beautiful,
we must carry it with us or we find it not.

August 8
A man's mind is like his car. If it gets to knocking too
much, he'd better have it overhauled or change it.

August 9
Do not speak of your happiness to one less fortunate than
yourself.

August 10
Humility is a strange thing. The minute you think you've
got it, you've lost it.

August 11
A foreigner is a friend I haven't met yet.

August 12
Habit is man's best friend or his worst enemy.

August 13
An unfailing mark of a blockhead is the chip on his shoulder.

August 14
Happiness is a perfume you cannot pour on others without getting a few drops on yourself.

August 15
A man's difficulties begin when he is able to do as he likes.

August 16
Be sure your brain is in gear before engaging your mouth.

August 17
To err may be human, but to admit it isn't.

August 18
They that know God will be humble; they that know themselves cannot be proud.

August 19
If you want to put the world right, start with yourself.

August 20
Friends are made by many acts—and lost by only one.

August 21
The greatest undeveloped territory in the world lies under your hat.

August 22
Laugh a little—love a little,
Skies are always blue!
Every cloud has silver linings,
But it's up to you!

August 23
You grow up the day you have your first real laugh—at yourself.

August 24
A man wrapped up in himself makes a very small bundle.

August 25
There is only one person with whom you can profitably compare yourself, and this person is your yesterday self: You.

August 26
Forgiveness is the fragrance the violet sheds on the heel that crushed it.

August 27
He that cannot forgive others breaks the bridge over which he must pass, for every man has need to be forgiven.

August 28
Education does not mean teaching people to know what they do not know; it means teaching them to behave as they do not behave.

August 29
In times of crisis we must avoid both ignorant change and ignorant opposition to change.

August 30
Any person who is always feeling sorry for himself,
should be.

August 31
The light of friendship is like the light of phosphorus,
seen when all around is dark.

September 1
Too many people quit looking for work when they find a
job.

September 2
Trouble is only opportunity in work clothes.

September 3
Work is the best narcotic.

September 4
The love you liberate in your work is the love you keep.

September 5
There is nothing permanent but change.

September 6
A college education seldom hurts a man if he's willing to
learn a little something after he graduates.

September 7
The greatest friend of truth is time,
And her constant companion is humility.

September 8
Education isn't play and it can't be made to look like
play. It is hard, hard work, but it can be made
interesting work.

September 9
A professor once said that it didn't matter if one said, 'I seed,' if one really had seen something.

September 10
Quite often when a man thinks his mind is getting broader it is only his conscience stretching.

September 11
The load of tomorrow added to that of yesterday, carried today, makes the strongest falter.

September 12
The aim of education is to enable man to continue his learning.

September 13
A college graduate is a person who had a chance to get an education.

September 14
A learned man has always wealth within himself.

September 15
Education should be as gradual as the moonrise, perceptible not in progress but in result.

September 16
Investment in knowledge pays the best interest.

September 17
What we do not understand we do not possess.

September 18
The purpose of education is to provide everyone with the opportunity to learn how best he may serve the world.

September 19
Teach thy tongue to say, 'I do not know.'

September 20
A teacher affects eternity; he can never tell where his influence stops.

September 21
If you don't scale the mountain, you can't see the view.

September 22
The diamond cannot be polished without friction, nor man perfected without trials.

September 23
Growing old is no more than a bad habit which a busy person has no time to form.

September 24
Men are wise in proportion not to their experience but to their capacity for experience.

September 25
The best thing for gray hair is a sensible head.

September 26
A man could retire nicely in his old age if he could dispose of his experience for what it cost him.

September 27
There is no place more delightful than one's own fireside.

September 28
Old age isn't so bad . . . when you consider the alternative.

September 29
I do not feel any age yet. There is no age to the spirit.

September 30
When you can no longer dwell in the solitude of your heart, you live in your lips and sound is a diversion and a pastime.

October 1
No wise man ever wished to be younger.

October 2
Without the *way*, there is no going;
Without the *truth*, there is no knowing;
Without the *life*, there is no living.

October 3
Be careful how you live; you may be the only Bible some people will ever read.

October 4
Cease to inquire what the future has in store, but take as a gift whatever the day brings forth.

October 5
The difference between stumbling blocks and stepping stones is the way a man uses them.

October 6
The smile on your face is the light in the window that tells people that you are at home.

October 7
Genius is only patience.

October 8
A man is not old until regrets take the place of dreams.

October 9
The highest reward for a man's toil is not what he gets for it, but rather what he becomes by it.

October 10
We are always complaining our days are few, and acting as though there would be no end of them.

October 11
We are all manufacturers, making goods, making trouble or making excuses.

October 12
No worlds left to conquer? The frontiers of the mind are just beginning to be discovered, and the spiritual world surrounding us yet remains a complete mystery.

October 13
Where there is an open mind, there will always be a frontier.

October 14
There is only a slight difference between keeping your chin up and sticking your neck out, but it's worth knowing.

October 15
Don't tell your friends about your *indigestion*: 'How are you' is a *greeting*, not a question.

October 16
I have noticed that folks are generally about as happy as they have made up their minds to be.

October 17
Almost all men improve on acquaintance.

October 18
One reason why a dog is such a lovable creature is that his tail wags instead of his tongue.

October 19
Living is like licking honey off a thorn.

October 20
No difficulties, no discovery,
No pains, no gains.

October 21
Work is love made visible.

October 22
To love life through labor is to be intimate with life's inmost secret.

October 23
Let us realize that what happens round us is largely outside our control, but that the way we choose to react to it is inside our control.

October 24
I have often regretted my speech, seldom my silence.

October 25
No echoes return to mock the silent tongue.

October 26
To admit I have been in the wrong is but saying that I am wiser today than I was yesterday.

October 27
Out of the mouths of babes come words we shouldn't have said in the first place.

October 28
Tact is the unsaid part of what you think.

October 29
We always weaken what we exaggerate.

October 30
True happiness depends upon close alliance with God.

October 31
It's all right to hold a conversation, but you should let go of it now and then.

November 1
I want a soul so full of joy—
Life's withering storms cannot destroy.

November 2
God never closes one door without opening another.

November 3
I can alter my life by altering my attitude of mind.

November 4
It takes the whole of life to learn how to live.

November 5
Heaven is blessed with perfect rest, but the blessing of earth is toil.

November 6
Instead of waiting upon the Lord, some people want the Lord to wait upon them.

November 7
Trying times are times for trying.

November 8
Perhaps the most valuable result of all education is the *ability* to make ourselves do the thing we have to do when it ought to be done, whether we like it or not.

November 9
Gossip is the art of saying nothing in a way that leaves nothing unsaid.

November 10
The night is not forever.

November 11
People are lonely because they build walls instead of bridges.

November 12
The light that shows us our sin is the light that heals us.

November 13
Happiness is a thing to be practiced like a violin.

November 14
Does your faith move mountains, or do mountains move your faith?

November 15
Prayer digs the channels from the reservoir of God's boundless resources to the tiny pools of our lives.

November 16
The secret of being miserable is to have the leisure to bother about whether you are happy or not.

November 17
If we pause to think, we will have cause to thank.

November 18
He only is advancing in life whose heart is getting softer, his blood warmer, his brain quicker, and his spirit entering into living peace.

November 19
You are not a reservoir with a limited amount of resources; you are a channel attached to unlimited divine resources.

November 20
If you would know the greatest sum in addition, count your blessings.

November 21
Some folks just don't seem to realize when they're moaning about not getting prayers answered, that NO is the answer.

November 22
A thankful heart is not only the greatest virtue, but the parent of all the other virtues.

November 23
Patience—in time the grass becomes milk.

November 24
The best way to succeed in life is to act on the advice you give to others.

November 25
I'm so glad I'm back home I'm glad I went.

November 26
Only the best behavior is good enough for daily use in the home.

November 27
'Yes, it's pretty hard,' the optimistic old woman admitted. 'I have to get along with only two teeth—one upper, one lower—but, thank goodness, they meet.'

November 28
Only one person in the whole wide world can defeat you. That is yourself!

November 29
It is better to understand a little than to misunderstand a lot.

November 30
This body is my house—it is not I.
Triumphant in this faith I live and die.

December 1
What I must do, and not what people think, is all that concerns me.

December 2
To will what God wills brings peace.

December 3
You can preach a better sermon with your life than with your lips.

December 4
Every noble life leaves the fibre of it interwoven in the woof of the world.

December 5
Money and time are the heaviest burdens of life, and the unhappiest of all mortals are those who have more of either than they know how to use.

December 6
A sad saint is a sorry saint.

December 7
All people smile in the same language.

December 8
Let us be the first to give a friendly sign, to nod first, smile first, speak first, and—if such a thing is necessary—forgive first.

December 9
Good depends not on things but on the use we make of things.

December 10
The only safe and sure way to destroy an enemy is to make him your friend.

December 11
Gratitude is the memory of the heart.

December 12
All that is necessary for the triumph of evil is that good men do nothing.

December 13
A mistake is evidence that someone has tried to do something.

December 14
There is nothing wrong with making mistakes, but don't respond to encores.

December 15
One on God's side is a majority.

December 16
I am to be so busy today that I must spend more time than usual in prayer.

December 17
The glory of life is to love, not to be loved, to give, not to get; to serve, not to be served.

December 18
Blessed is the man who digs a well from which another may draw faith.

December 19
Spilled on this earth are all the joys of heaven.

December 20
Whoever has resigned himself to fate, will find that fate accepts his resignation.

December 21
Even moderation ought not to be practiced to excess.

December 22
Climb the mountains and get their glad tidings. Nature's peace will flow to you as the sunshine flows into the trees. The winds blow their own freshness into you, and the storms their energy, while cares drop away from you like the leaves of autumn.

December 23
Joy is not in things, it is in us.

December 24
Mirth is from God, and dullness is from the devil. You can never be too sprightly, you can never be too good-tempered.

December 25
In His will is our peace.

December 26
May you live all the days of your life.

December 27
We may give without loving, but we cannot love without giving.

December 28
For when the One Great Scorer comes,
To write against your name,
He writes not that you lost or won,
But how you played the game.

December 29
Be cheerful. Of all the things you wear, your expression is the most important.

December 30
A wish is a desire without any attempt to attain its end.

December 31
All problems become smaller if you don't dodge them but confront them. Touch a thistle timidly and it will prick you; grasp it boldly and its spines crumble.

The material in this book has
been collected over a long period
of time. Many of the original
sources are unknown to the compiler.
The compiler wishes to acknowledge
the original authors, whoever they
may be, but has confidence that
they would urge, with her, "Do not
inquire as to who said this, but
pay attention to what is said."

Cover designed by Adair Wilson
Designed by Mansfield Drowne
Type style is Melior